Praise for

HOW TO CONNECT WITH DONORS
AND DOUBLE THE MONEY YOU RAISE

"Story by story, this book is brimming with wisdom. Inspiring but practical, rooted in long experience but immediately applicable, it proves Tom's point: that fundraising is all about building relationships."

Rushworth M. Kidder, President
Institute for Global Ethics
Trustee, Charles Stewart Mott Foundation

"Tom Wolf focuses on the relationship side of fundraising, and therefore provides welcome relief as the craft becomes increasingly metric-oriented – the number of calls, meetings, asks. He provides great encouragement to use more imagination, time, and care in connecting to people."

Christine W. Letts, Senior Associate Dean
Rita E. Hauser Senior Lecturer in the Practice of
Philanthropy and Nonprofit Leadership
Harvard Kennedy School

"*How to Connect with Donors* provides us with the insights we all need to be at our best and at our most effective. Tom gives us his best with a light and humorous touch."

Tony Woodcock, President
New England Conservatory

"With colorful and provocative stories Tom Wolf reminds us that fundraising is an art not a science. It is about people, not about institutions. When did you last enjoy a book about asking people for money?"

Michael Marsicano, President and CEO
Foundation for the Carolinas

D0064500

Thomas Wolf

How to Connect With Donors

And Double the Money You Raise

January 14, 2012

FOREWORD BY

Hodding Carter

Emerson
& Church
PUBLISHERS

Dear Kathy,
I hope this book helps your
work as you inspire donors to
be generous and thankful for
their God Given
abundance.
It is a pleasure to be working
with you. Peace, Love and Joy,
Charles +

First printed in January 2011

Printed in the United States of America

ISBN 978-1-889102-42-9

10 9 8 7 6 5 4 3 2 1

This text is printed on acid-free paper.

> *Copies of this book are available from the
> publisher at discount when purchased in
> quantity for boards of directors or staff.*

Emerson & Church, Publishers
15 Brook Street • Medfield, MA 02052
Tel. 508-359-0019 • www.emersonandchurch.com

Library of Congress Cataloging-in-Publication Data

Wolf, Thomas.
  How to connect with donors and double the money you raise / by
Thomas Wolf.
    p. cm.
ISBN 1-889102-42-3 (pbk. : alk. paper)
  1. Fund raising. I. Title.
HV41.2.W65 2011
  658.15'224—dc22
                                    2010037562

FOREWORD

When it comes to money, it is easier to give than it is to seek. You need look no further than my record as a fundraiser to prove the point. Man and boy, I have been very, very bad at it, whether asking local merchants to support my senior class trip almost 60 years ago or asking the Ford Foundation to support an international exchange program in the midst of the Cold War. Grinding my teeth with fear and loathing, I failed far more often than I succeeded.

While it is cold comfort, it turns out that I have not been alone. Asking someone else for money is an unnatural act for many of us, a fact of human nature that complicates life for nonprofit organizations. Soliciting money, whether from friends, strangers, or near-anonymous institutions, is what they must do to survive. Doing it well is not something that comes naturally.

To navigate this conundrum, you could not ask for a better guide than the pages that follow. Tom Wolf's distilled wisdom about connecting with donors comes from a man who has been a fundraising professional, a nonprofit leader, and a foundation executive. That could have meant this slim volume would be as boring as dry toast or as stimulating as sermons in an unknown tongue. Instead, it is warm, witty, insightful, immensely practical and engrossing from start to finish.

My one regret is that Tom did not write it long ago, when I was beginning a long avocational career as a man with a tin cup. But it's never too late to learn, not even for me, when your teacher is as grounded in his subject as he is passionate about its objectives.

Transparency requires that I say that the Wolfs and the Carters have been friends for over a half century. As a result, I recognize many of the people and stories that stud his chapters and illustrate his points.

But even if I didn't, they would resonate, as they probably will with most of you. Whatever our backgrounds, we are likely to have been in similar situations, to have known our own versions of Tom Wolf's exemplars, and absorbed the lessons of cautionary tales akin to his.

And that is his central point. When it comes to fundraising, what is crucial to the outcome are the human relationships that inform it. His advice begins and ends with a compelling proposition: Fundraising at root is all about human beings and their interests, not mission statements and flow charts. It's about connections established over time and discourse based on mutual interest.⟩

And therein lies the secret of Tom Wolf's accomplishment. A human being talks to us from the pages of a how-to treatise. He shares triumphs and flops, misunderstandings and insights. He does not lecture; he illustrates. He does not detach from complexity; he plunges into it and calmly suggests ways out.

If you pull back just a little from the narrative flow, you understand something else. Tom Wolf's stated mission is to help us improve our ability to persuade people to give money to worthy causes. This, to repeat, he does to extraordinary effect by enlisting a natural storyteller's skills to give life to his rare depth of practical experience. But while his talking points are shaped to a vocational end, they are no less a roadmap to perfecting human interaction and human connection. To put it another way, the cultivated civility and consideration that he commends to the fundraiser is the sine qua non for the reconstruction of a truly civil society in our deeply fractured nation.

In all of this, I hear his mother's voice and see her face. Irene Wolf made everyone who met her believe they were of special merit; believing it, they were. And I see and hear no less my own mother, so akin to Irene and so much of the same generation though of radically different background and experience. Theirs was an outward manifestation of an inner reality: each believed in the intrinsic worth of others. Not coincidentally, they were extraordinarily successful in creating, guiding, and sustaining nonprofit organizations, dreaming big dreams and finding the money to give them life.

Few of us can measure up to Irene Wolf's incandescent spirit. Most of us will never have Tom Wolf's wealth of experience. But the fact-based, situation-located advice that he offers, its message arising from his commitment to our shared humanity, is there for the taking. Put to use, it can change fundraising from a chore to an inspired calling.

Hodding Carter   *Chapel Hill, North Carolina*

INTRODUCTION

A few years ago, I was invited to a party where the only person I knew was the host. My wife was away so I was on my own.

After greeting the host and ordering a drink, I steeled myself for what promised to be a long evening. At that moment, a young man came up and introduced himself. "You're Tom Wolf," he said. "I've always wanted to meet you. If you have a moment, I'd love you to come over here and meet some of my friends."

Later, I learned that the host had deputized a group of people to act as a welcoming crew and my new friend was simply doing his job. Did I feel manipulated? Not at all. It was a wonderful evening and I met many new and interesting people.

When the party's host sent me a fundraising letter the next year, he referred to the evening and said how much his young friend had enjoyed meeting me. I didn't hesitate before putting a check in the return envelope.

For years, I've taught fundraising. I've presented scores of fundraising seminars and workshops and taught a class on the subject at Harvard University. My students included both beginners and people who had been in the field for several years.

In these sessions, I focused on the technicalities of raising money. We discussed how to write a good annual fund letter, how to design a capital campaign, and how to organize a development department. I encouraged people to learn about charitable remainder trusts and pooled income funds and, of course, how to construct a winning foundation proposal.

But over the years, I noticed something striking. On the first day of class – before ever presenting any of this material – I could predict with a fair degree of accuracy who was going be an effective fundraiser and who wasn't.

It had less to do with the knowledge they carried into class and much more to do with how they interacted with me and their peers. If they looked me in the eye, offered a firm handshake, and steered the conversation away from themselves and toward the person whom they were speaking with, I knew they had mastered a large part of the technique. The best ones listened, asked questions, and smiled.

For a long time, I've wanted to explore this fascinating interpersonal side of fundraising. Other books (including some of my own) focus on techniques and strategies. The thrust of this book is different. It explores various ways to build strong relationships, draw donors closer to you, and in the process, make them more than names on a prospect list.

To make the book most personal, I will share stories (some a bit embarrassing from this so-called expert) based on my own experience and those of friends and acquaintances.

Before beginning, let's agree that some individuals are born with a knack for making other people like them, and this gives them a head start as fundraisers. Others, the shyer types, may feel it's impossible to become a gregarious "hail-fellow-well-met" person who always seems to charm others (including, of course, big donors).

And that's exactly the way I felt when I began. I just didn't think I had the personality or the energy to become a skilled fundraiser. But let's remember that Dale Carnegie, decades ago, made a fortune teaching shy and retiring people that they could develop into good salesmen and public speakers. Fundraising is no different. Even introverts can become great fundraisers. Of course it takes practice. But it can be done.

As I've always said to my students at the beginning of our time together, "You're looking at a guy who was by nature uncomfortable with people. But if you watch me with a donor, you'd never know it. If I could learn, so can you."

So come join the adventure. I trust you'll have some fun ... and a few laughs along the way.

For Simon

A Personal Note
from the Author

This book is based on a long career of raising money, including 30 years of advising other people how to do it. Over the years, many things have changed in the world of fundraising. But not the essential fact that our relationships with donors often determine just how generous they will be.

Some of the stories in this book trumpet successes. But many describe my failures too. Any effective and honest fundraiser has both tales to tell.

The people in this book are real – every one of them. Occasionally I've changed a name to protect the anonymity of a treasured donor. Then, too, I don't want to embarrass those who from time to time may have looked, well, somewhat foolish.

Because the book is about relating to donors – at times befriending them – an obvious concern is whether the whole connecting process smacks of some manipulative ploy to snare money from the unsuspecting.

There's an easy answer to this.

When we're inauthentic, donors can tell. Even if I had the perfect system for pretending, it wouldn't work for very long. And the opposite is also true. When we conduct ourselves with integrity, it shines through, especially as donors come to know us through the years.

So don't worry. This isn't about compromising your ethics, it's about being yourself. In my early fundraising years I often tried to be what I thought donors wanted me to be. It didn't work. What they liked was a real person who was simply himself.

Thomas Wolf   *Cambridge, Massachusetts*

CONTENTS

FOREWORD
INTRODUCTION
PERSONAL NOTE FROM THE AUTHOR

1	I'd love to get to know you better	17
2	Enough about me!	23
3	What's wrong with talking about money?	31
4	It's the donor's ballgame	35
5	Thank you. Thank you. Thank you!	43
6	Remember the children	49
7	Can you be too close to ask?	55
8	Why isn't he giving?!	61
9	When donors disappoint	69
10	Recovering from a fumble	77
11	But I can't stand the fellow!	83
12	Whose friend are you anyway?	89
13	We honor his memory	93
14	Grantmakers need attention too	99

AFTERWORD

1

I'd Love to Get to Know You Better

"It's all about turning a name into a relationship." So said one of my mentors, the late Francis Bosworth, executive director of a settlement house in Philadelphia.

Boz, as he was affectionately called, was a superb fundraiser – a schmoozer, something of a gossip, and people loved being around him.

Each year, the list of donors to the Friends Neighborhood Guild would grow. Yet never in all the years I knew him did I ever catch Boz at his desk (though it was said he spent many hours there). When I saw him, he was out in the community, expanding his circle, charming people.

Boz was the consummate master of relationship

building or, as many people call it, "friendraising." He had the ability to get to know people and a special knack for turning those acquaintances into committed supporters. And watching him do it was marvelous fun.

Boz's organization wasn't the stylish kind that attracts big donors. It was located in one of the less desirable parts of the city, surrounded by neither fancy restaurants nor great architecture. Indeed, many of the buildings in the neighborhood were dilapidated.

Nor did the Guild offer the social panache of a symphony orchestra or art museum. Its programs were about basic human needs – food, housing, education, safety – and many of its constituents were poor. Among them were recent immigrants wanting to learn English so they could find jobs.

Indeed, that's how Boz managed to involve my mother with his organization. He met Irene at a party and rather than answer her initial questions about his work, he used his inimitable charm to learn about *her* background.

Irene was born in Russia and spoke several languages. She often served as a foreign language guide at the local art museum. Boz drew her out as she told amusing stories about her more colorful "clients."

Then Boz mentioned in passing that there was a little known immigrant population in Philadelphia – the

Kalmyks – who were served by his organization. Did she know about these Russian-speaking people?

Many of them yearned to learn English and Boz was on the lookout for native Russian speakers. If Irene would ever consider being a guest teacher at the Guild, Boz was sure the students would love to meet her, even if she only came once or twice.

"You have so many fascinating stories to tell," he said. Boz didn't push hard but he managed to convince Irene to come and visit. And when she did, he made sure she was treated like a celebrity. In fact she had such a good time she decided to teach a few classes.

The approach was classic Boz. Surely he considered Irene a fundraising prospect. But he never mentioned money. In fact, she was well into her second year of volunteering before he even asked for her first gift. By that time, she was totally committed to Boz, the Guild, and her students.

Boz thus completed the second part of the friendraising loop, taking an acquaintance and transforming her into a beloved member of his organizational family. She in turn became a donor and a fundraiser on his behalf.

In teaching me the elements of "friendraising," Boz counseled patience coupled with genuine interest. "The contributions will come in time (or they won't). But that isn't the place to begin. Never ask a stranger for a large gift."

This latter advice was a bit of an exaggeration, of course. We request donations from plenty of people we don't know (and often are successful doing so). If we had to know each of our donors personally, our organizations would wither.

But in an age when fundraising books and courses teach the science and metrics of list building, Boz's empathic wisdom was an important complement for two reasons. First, it was built on the idea that prospect lists take on much greater value when the names become flesh-and-blood people; and, second, that a major benefit of this approach is that it so often results in turning the casual small donor into an intensely loyal and large one.

Boz taught me another valuable lesson in the art of friendraising and, ironically, it involved, once again, my own extended family. My father's relatives had settled in Philadelphia during the second half of the 19th century. They were prolific – having produced numerous offspring who became involved in the law, banking, local businesses, the rare book trade, and in one case, politics (a state senator). Many were also active in philanthropy and Boz knew my mother offered valuable access to what was an A-list of prospects.

But his approach was cautious. He never asked Irene to solicit any of her husband's relatives – a good thing too, since there was a family proscription against it.

Though Irene personalized countless fundraising letters for Boz, none ever went to a member of the family. That said, what she did do was provide valuable information about uncles, cousins, and brothers-in law – what their interests were, what charities they supported, what activities their children were involved in, where their children went to school.

In addition, she often included Boz at gatherings where he could get acquainted with family members. His ability to draw them out and show interest in their favorite activities was uncanny (or so it seemed to them). Most were unsuspecting that much information had been provided in advance by my mother.

The lesson here is simple but one I so often missed. Sometimes the direct approach in fundraising isn't the best; working a connection quietly and behind the scenes is. In the past decade, I've been reminded of this lesson again and again. I see many trustees and volunteers bristling at the pressure placed on them to be more aggressive in tapping their friends and relatives. Often it seems like an either/or dilemma – either they "make the asks" or they fail to fulfill their responsibilities.

Boz showed there was a third way – an indirect approach that may be best for everyone involved. It allows people to be helpful while not putting them in the position of jeopardizing key relationships. Boz never let his trustees and volunteers off the hook. But he always managed to find a comfortable way for them to succeed.

2

Enough About Me!

Remember the gag about two people who see each other after many years? The first blathers on and on about the things she's done, her various marriages, her plastic surgery, her pets, her friends, and her enemies. After 20 minutes, she says, "Enough about me, what about you? What do *you* think of me?"

I wish there were a training film for fundraisers that put this gag front and center so they could see how counterproductive it is. Even those of us who are wise enough to avoid a soliloquy about ourselves can make the same mistake when talking endlessly about our organization.

Isn't that what you're supposed to be doing? Talking about your organization?

Well, yes and no.

As Peter, one of my early mentors taught me, a

fundraising call – especially an initial one – is primarily an opportunity to form or deepen a relationship. And ironically, the best way to be remembered is to let your prospect do the talking.

"Think about the people you like to spend time with," says Peter. "Are they the ones who constantly focus the conversation on themselves or those who show interest in you?"

Peter continues: "Would that every fundraiser took a crash course in empathy! Call it the art of good listening. It's often the difference between success and failure."

Since it sets the tone and helps to form your prospect's initial impression, good listening is especially key at the beginning of a fundraising call. I learned that the hard way.

As the young director of the newly formed New England Foundation for the Arts, my board wanted me to explore the possibility of raising funds from regional corporations (which we would then redistribute as grants).

I'd never done corporate fundraising so I hired Peter, both to help me raise money and also to teach me whatever special techniques there were to master.

His method was to begin with two "informational interviews" – opportunities to "seek advice" on setting up the new program. At these meetings, Peter was a master at drawing out each individual, listening to what he or she had to say, and subtly injecting a few timely phrases about how our program might be perfect for addressing the particular corporation's agenda.

BAD

Then it was my turn to lead. I boned up for a few hours before our next meeting, preparing myself with facts and figures and accomplishments. And only minutes into the meeting it all came spewing forth.

I couldn't help myself. I was sure I was dazzling. But once we left the building, Peter was furious. "So what do you know about Mr. Kerner's corporation?" he asked. "What would the company be interested in funding? What are Kerner's personal interests? What is he excited about? Who's he going to help you see next?"

I had to agree. I left with little more than I'd come with.

Days later it was Peter's turn again. We secured a meeting with Ruth, a long-time giving officer from a storied corporation in Boston. "Don't say anything unless I kick you under the table," said Peter. "And keep your answers to a few sentences."

We arrived and Peter immediately went over to some photos on Ruth's desk. "What attractive kids! Are they yours?"

"Yes," said Ruth. "They're grown now, but I love these pictures so I keep them here."

"And what are they up to now?" he asked. Understand, Peter is genuinely interested in people, so there was no guile to his words.

Ruth then launched into a discussion of her kids. One, it turned out, was an educator with an interest in the arts.

"That's a coincidence," said Peter. "That's one of the things we came here to talk about – the arts. Tom's running a program now that I bet is right up her alley."

I got my first kick from Peter under the table and briefly described the program.

Ruth's other child was in the Peace Corps in Africa training local residents in various forms of community building.

Peter again made the connection. "One of the things we've found through the program Tom's running is that technical assistance and training can be more valuable than direct grants. Tom, tell Ruth about the one you're running."

My second cue. I spoke briefly and this time hit pay dirt. Ruth got excited and, heeding Peter's earlier counsel, I simply listened as Ruth spoke. "You know, as a giving officer of a corporation that prides itself on professional development, I've always wondered whether we should be funding workshops and training. So many of the organizations applying to us aren't good candidates for our program grants."

This was the magic moment. And over the years I've come to look for and savor those instances in conversations when donors wonder if maybe, just maybe, you can help them solve *their* problems or carry out *their* agenda. In this case, the story has a happy ending. Ruth gave us $15,000 to develop training materials and was so thrilled with the result she became an ongoing donor.

Now, contrast our meeting with Ruth with the following.

A few years back I was asked to conduct a fundraising workshop at a local university. My audience was a partially student-run organization that places student volunteers in community settings. I knew of the group and loved the idea of working with students who would themselves one day be trustees and perhaps staff of nonprofit organizations.

I was offered an honorarium, but challenged the students to raise it back from me. If they did well, I'd add more cash in the bargain.

During the session, I described myself as a prospect and hinted that they ought to think about applying their skills to someone like me, a person who was well disposed toward their organization and in a position to give.

A week later, I received a call from one of the students who asked if she could come see me as a follow-up to the session. She would bring someone with her (the name didn't ring a bell) and they'd like to continue the learning process and get some more advice. Not a bad start, I thought.

The visit turned out to be anything but a success. The person accompanying the student was a so-called "professional," a member of the staff. My desire was to interact with students, as I had told the group initially, but it was the staff member who droned on and on.

At one point I said, "I'm quite familiar with the program you're describing," but the hint was lost in his barrage of words. I tried to draw out the student who was sitting off to the side, but that too failed to have an impact.

Finally, I walked over to my computer. "I suppose you have online giving. How much do you want?" They named a figure. I made the contribution and said I had another meeting. They left the office and I'm sure they felt it had gone well. Hardly. I vowed never again to make a contribution to the group.

In recounting these stories to students who want to become skilled fundraisers, I refer them to one of my favorite quotes by the great English novelist, Thomas Hardy: "That man's silence is wonderful to listen to."

"Be like that man," I tell them.

3

What's Wrong with Talking About Money?

If I were to choose one potential donor I'd like to make friends with, it would be the wealthy individual who says (or implies) that he or she doesn't want to talk about money and effectively doesn't want to be solicited.

If I could choose another, it would be an existing donor (perhaps a board member) who could be giving at a much higher level but also doesn't want to discuss personal philanthropy.

That was my dilemma with the late Roland Burden-Muller, an elegant gentleman who insisted that I, the director of a small organization he supported, should never ask him for money. Instead, I could come to his seaside "cottage" (in reality an old-fashioned mansion) for a five-course luncheon at the end of the fiscal year and review how things had gone.

These meals, which inevitably lasted several hours, were cooked by his French chef and served by his butler. Ostensibly the time was to be spent in friendly chat and we'd touch on various subjects before he'd invite me to have coffee on the porch, gazing at the islands in Maine's Penobscot Bay.

This annual lunch was my one opportunity to talk about the organization's needs. It wasn't an "ask" *per se* but it met his rules. His generosity when I followed his protocol made his non-solicitation request easy to honor.

In thinking about it years later, I suspect that Burden-Muller was lonely. He had few friends in the area and the conversation obviously was something he looked forward to. His insistence on the lunch – rather than a letter – was a form of reaching out for a small measure of human interaction.

People like Burden-Muller are a pleasure to deal with. But what happens when there aren't any established rules and a "Do Not Solicit" message appears to be just that?

Perhaps the most challenging donor I've ever dealt with – and easily one of the most generous – was the late Harvey Picker. Harvey was a remarkable man whose career had spanned business, medicine, foreign service, and nonprofit trusteeship, among many activities.

Because Harvey was wealthy and generous, people lined up to ask him for money ... all the time. I'm sure it was wearisome for him. What I soon learned was that I'd never get money if I asked for it. As he told us many times, he didn't need or want to be solicited. For many years, this wasn't a problem because he was meticulous in his annual support.

However, when it came to larger gifts for special occasions and needs, I was in a quandary. How to ask became a real challenge. The solution came to me by accident.

At the time, Harvey was on the board of our music organization and uncharacteristically had missed a meeting. I asked whether it would be okay if I stopped by to brief him. I also needed his advice on a particular matter. Harvey had far more nonprofit experience than I or any of my other board members and the request was sincere. Harvey was delighted – it seemed he loved giving advice and he suggested an afternoon cruise on his sailboat.

I went over the agenda and then mentioned a discussion item that was unresolved – what we should do about our struggle to keep our radio shows on the air. "We have to supply the material in a format the station can broadcast. Unfortunately they've changed their technology and can't play our tapes anymore. Unless we update all of our material, we're off the air."

Harvey: "How much would it cost to convert the tapes?"

Tom: "Well, we have a backlog. If we did everything it would be about $15,000."

Harvey: "That doesn't sound like much. Why don't you send me a letter, one page, describing what you need and why and I'll see what I can do."

What started through this fortuitous accident ended in a tradition. Periodically, especially after Harvey left the board, I would visit, update him, and seek his counsel. Sometimes I left only with advice. Other times, I left with advice and a check.

Many have told me that they too encounter donors who respond to the request for advice with money, which is proof positive of the old adage – told to me originally by capital campaign consultant, Bob Demont – "Ask people for money, they give you advice; ask them for advice, they give you money."

4

It's the Donor's Ballgame

A little old man shuffles up to the ticket office at
the University of Michigan and asks whether he might
buy a ticket for the big game with Ohio State the next
day. "Something near the 50 yard line would be nice,"
he says.

The ticket seller guffaws. "There hasn't been a ticket
available for that game for weeks ... *anywhere* in the
stadium."

"Okay," the little man says and walks away.

About an hour later, the athletic director and the
football coach are summoned to an emergency
meeting. The President is apoplectic. "An alum just
walked into my office a few minutes ago and is talking
about giving the University a hundred million dollars.
In our conversation, he mentioned that he couldn't
get a ticket to the Ohio State game tomorrow. I don't

care if you have to bounce the President of the United States or the Pope, give him anything he wants."

By the time the little man returns to the ticket office, the band has been assembled and they're playing the school song. The athletic director apologizes for the previous error and says, "There was a misunderstanding. Of course we have a ticket for you – the seat is in the President's box, will that suffice?"

"Well I don't want to put you to any trouble, but that would be fine."

"And the President's limo will pick you up and bring you to a special brunch before the game. Will that be okay?"

"Yes, very nice and much too generous," is his modest answer.

"And is there anything else we can do for you?"

"Well can you tell me when the game starts?"

"What time would you like it to start?" asks the athletic director.

This delicious, over-the-top story makes an important point – if you want to be successful with donors, give them what they want (assuming you can, of course).

Start with the easy stuff – a birthday card, a note of congratulations when a child graduates, a get-well note when the donor is sick. Then there are other small gifts that can make a big difference – the more personal the better.

In the summer, for example, I make homemade vinegar with herbs from our family garden and concoct an apple rose-hip sauce from our orchard. I make little gifts of these for friends, including some donors. I enjoy doing it and because the gifts are totally unnecessary, they give the recipients obvious pleasure.

In some cases, a donor may request a favor – one that could provide a special opportunity for you. "Any chance you can get a ticket to your sold-out opening for my friend Bob?" "Could someone at the office give me a lift to the board meeting?" "I wonder if one of your curators would come with me to a gallery as I'm thinking about buying a particular painting."

In each of these cases, the favor may simply be a way of doing something nice or it may lead to more substantial long-term results. Friend Bob may be another prospect. The lift to the board meeting might be a chance to talk about a special project needing funding. The trip to the gallery may result in a painting that ultimately is bequeathed to the curator's institution. Whether or not any of these things happen, the nice gesture will certainly be remembered and probably reciprocated in some way.

But the question of how to cater to donors' wishes

takes on a different cast when the request directly impacts your organizational activities. Sometimes a donor may want you to hire a friend or family member, or take on a new program, or build something. That poses no problem if these are things you're going to do anyway. But sometimes it's a little more complicated. The request may actually run counter to your plans or policies.

One of my own greatest regrets was hiring an individual based on the urging of a donor. Not only was the decision wrong initially, but undoing it alienated the donor far more than simply saying I'd take his opinions into account when we looked at the candidates.

At other times the dilemma of trying to please (or appease) a donor emanates from a situation over which the organization has no control. My friend Barbara Bentley, who for many years has headed the Friends of Baxter State Park in Maine, told me of one such situation.

"We have a generous member who carefully reads all our minutes and publications and then asks if he might help out, make our lives a little easier by helping us to pay for such and such. He loves to identify the project and then write a check. He's done this a number of times, and of course we're grateful.

"But although the Park we support is an independent entity, it's regulated by the State of Maine and we're not allowed to earmark gifts. Our donor has always found this hard to understand. For close to 25 years, he tried to give a large sum for trails and maintenance but wasn't able to make it work legally. Then, during the Katahdin Lake Campaign a few years back, the Governor and Attorney General got together – when time to raise the necessary millions was running out – and figured out a legal vehicle for accepting almost $10 million from this gentleman for a designated purpose."

Wow, you might say. That's a no-brainer! What took them so long? Of course they should have done what the donor wanted. But the issue was a legal one and the complex actions were only worthwhile once it was clear that an extraordinary gift was in the offing.

Yet even when a gift is large, the situation isn't always so clear cut. Sometimes what the donor wants is simply not in the best interests of the organization. One of my mentors was Boris Goldovsky, whose eponymous Goldovsky Opera Theatre was supported by many public and private funders. In training me, he recounted what he called his "least favorite fundraising story."

"I remember sitting down with people from a major

foundation who told me they were willing to give a six figure gift if I'd undertake a national tour of the opera 'Carmen.' In my heart I knew it wasn't right for us – the production was too big given the size of the gift – but I took the money anyway because it was a prestigious foundation.

"It was the largest gift in the Opera's history. I wanted to list the foundation in our group of supporters, so I told myself it would all work out in the end. But I was wrong. It didn't work out. A year later was the only time in 40 years the Opera came close to bankruptcy and all because of a gift I shouldn't have taken."

In such cases, how do you say no in a way that doesn't leave a sour taste in a donor's mouth? Irene was a master at this.

At a dinner party one evening, she was describing an organization for which she volunteered to a slightly inebriated elderly gent.

"Brilliant, brilliant," he'd exclaim every few minutes, often interrupting her in mid-sentence, and then, "I have a great idea how I could help." He launched into a slightly incoherent description of a totally inappropriate idea for a program. I caught Irene's eye and smiled as if to say, "Let's see how you get out of this." Meanwhile the gentleman claimed to have a blank check in his wallet and was prepared to write it out on the spot.

"How wonderful," exclaimed Irene. "You are truly inspired. And I hope someday our organization will have matured to the point where we can accept such a gift. If we took it now, we couldn't possibly do your idea justice. But I can't tell you how grateful I am. You've given me such good ideas to bring back to the board to inspire them and I will mention this at our next meeting."

I don't know whether it is what she said or how she said it (or both), but the irony is that despite turning down the donor's request, Irene received his generous gift anyway.

5

Thank You. Thank You. Thank You!

There's no question that it's from Aunt Cupid (yes, her real name) I inherited my obsession with thank you notes. Cupid was a generous purveyor of presents – at birthdays, at holidays, and on special occasions. And she expected well-reared children to thank her for them ... promptly, and in writing.

In the competition for who had the best-raised children, my mother would be furious when she received a call saying, "I sent a present to Tommy for his birthday. I haven't heard anything so I wondered whether he received it." Of course that was code for the real message about the merits of Tommy's upbringing.

Prompt thank you notes were drilled into me from

a young age and it turned out to be a boon. I got good at it, realizing that for those who gave often, a generic letter wouldn't do. And the more I customized the letter, the more praise I received. When years later I became a nonprofit board member and executive, I applied this lesson practically without modification and invariably with good results.

Just as people remember when someone takes the time to write a warm and obviously personal thank you, they also remember when you don't. I think back on my experience with the Mount Auburn Hospital in Cambridge, Massachusetts.

In 1976, my six-year-old daughter, Lea, was in a gym class at Cambridge Friends School and accidentally landed head first against a brick wall while playing an indoor soccer game. She was unconscious for a while and by the time my wife and I received the news, an ambulance was speeding her to Mount Auburn Hospital.

From the moment she was admitted to the time, hours later, when she was released with a clean bill of health, everything about the experience was superb. She received rapid and quality care, all the necessary tests were done, the nurses were solicitous and knew how to handle a child (and her nervous parents). Everyone made us feel calm.

Two days later, I called the hospital and made sure I had the correct spelling of each doctor and nurse who had seen Lea. I then wrote a long letter thanking each by name, describing what they'd done and thanking the hospital for the quality care my daughter received. I also inserted in the envelope a check for $250. A week later, I received a form letter acknowledging the gift.

Now it's true that everything about this transaction was "correct" from the hospital's point of view. They had delivered quality service, they had received what for a hospital was a modest gift, and they had generated an acknowledgement. Most nonprofits have a giving level that triggers more personalized acknowledgement and I hadn't cleared that threshold.

But the hospital system missed one important step. The letter was clearly from a *very* enthusiastic user of the hospital, the zip code on the return envelope would have indicated the capacity to give more, and someone on the development staff could easily have jotted a note telling me that my messages of appreciation had been conveyed to the appropriate staff.

Perhaps I could (or should) have rung up the hospital's development office and expressed my disapproval. Probably some well-intentioned person was simply following procedure and my call might have prompted the development staff to rethink how the department operates. As my wife pointed out, that would have been more productive than holding a grudge for 20 years.

But a donor ignored can become a curmudgeon with no sense of forgiveness. There is a predictable sense of disappointment when the organization is too busy to acknowledge, even in a small way, a heartfelt letter, but not too busy to put the donor in the database and generate a letter later asking for more money.

Even though I was plenty peeved, the hospital might still have recovered from its mistake. I'm a strong believer in finding out *why* a donor stops giving. At the end of the fiscal year, I make a list of lapsed donors and send out a letter saying, "We're trying to do better and would love your help in understanding where we can improve."

A simple survey with a self-addressed stamped return envelope gives donors the opportunity to indicate why they've stopped giving. A 30 to 50 percent response rate isn't unusual for such a mailing and, surprisingly, many include a check.

Had I received such a survey and detailed my complaint, I suspect someone from the development office would have called. I would have blown off some steam and, sufficiently satisfied, continued my support for years.

The final lesson on thank you notes comes from the all-time champion of the genre, Polly Chatfield. Polly is part of a generous family whose philanthropic activities include gifts for land conservation, youth development, and the arts, among other causes. Polly herself is generous and that includes throwing herself wholeheartedly into the fundraising process for organizations for which she volunteers. I don't know which I like receiving more – her fundraising request letters or her thank you letters when such a gift is sent. Each is personal, handwritten, and heartfelt.

I always wondered whether her letters might be just a little generic – they were so good. Then one week I received two thank you notes from Polly for the same gift. It was one of those easy-to-make mistakes when someone is in note-writing mode and neglects to tick off a name after acknowledging a gift. That's clearly what happened to Polly and the receipt of the second note floored me. Her first note was wonderful. Her second was even better ... and completely different! Anyone who can be that spontaneous and creative deserves special commendation in my Fundraisers Hall of Fame.

I'll close with a question I'm sometimes asked: "Does email suffice for a thank you note?" In the old days (a few years ago), I would have automatically answered no. But with so many people online today, I suggest applying what I call the Aunt Cupid test. How would Aunt Cupid (as representing the person giving the gift) feel? I suspect it depends very much on the donor. My default is pen, paper, and stamp. But every rule is made to be broken ... sometimes.

6

Remember the Children

After decades of fundraising, I'm sometimes asked, "What's the worst mistake you've made in your career?" It's a question I can answer without hesitation because the mistake is one I made not just once, but countless times ... and at great cost. Simply put, I didn't pay enough attention to my donors' children.

Don't get me wrong. I've spent more hours than I'd care to admit bouncing little Johnny on my knee or listening to Missy play the piano. I've paid my share of fulsome compliments to donors about the extraordinary qualities of their children and their grandchildren. That kind of behavior is a given and anyone who misses the opportunity to praise a donor's offspring probably lacks the temperament of a good fundraiser.

But as the years have passed, I've come to realize

that noticing and complimenting children isn't enough – at least not for the long term. All that effort, I finally understood, is aimed at making the *donors* happy. It has nothing to do with fostering an enduring relationship with the children. And this can be a missed opportunity of colossal proportions.

Needless to say, donors age and in time leave us. For those with a good deal of money, much of their wealth will live on after them. Where there are children, it's the younger generation who will ultimately control where the family philanthropic dollars are directed.

I'm not suggesting we cultivate friendships with six-year-olds. But youngsters turn into young adults quickly and establish their own philanthropic preferences. When their parents' estates are finally passed on, the kids in many cases have already established loyalties to organizations different from the ones their parents supported. Simply put, befriending the children can help prevent the family philanthropy from straying once the parents are gone.

Surprisingly, even when a family foundation is involved, the children don't always respect the preferences of their deceased parents. For years I worked with Valerie who had created a foundation independent of her husband for the very reason that she was interested in areas he wasn't.

Valerie had a clear pattern of giving with which her children were familiar (they had participated in many of the grantmaking decisions as co-trustees). Surely, I thought, they would continue supporting her favorite charities as a way of honoring her memory.

But Valerie was dead less than a year when her foundation turned to new organizations that were of interest to her children but didn't really align with Valerie's interests. Quite frankly, I was shocked and felt personally betrayed. I was sure this situation was an anomaly and that other children behaved with more respect until I saw the pattern repeated again and again.

Not all children are so iconoclastic, however. In fact with Pete I was luckier. His mother, Elsie, was one of my most generous – and idiosyncratic – donors. Originally a modest contributor to the music organization I was running at the time, I received a call from her one afternoon asking why a visiting pianist had used his own piano for a concert.

"Well to be truthful," I said, "our concert grand just isn't up to his standards." Elsie's response was immediate. "Then I'm going to give you a new one that's as good as they come." I hinted that tens of thousands of dollars would be involved. "That's fine," she said, and a few months later she wrote out a check.

Her son Pete was someone I got to know well over

the ensuing years and we became good friends. As Elsie aged and he took over her finances, Pete, who by now was interested in our work too, was scrupulous about making sure her philanthropic support continued in a way she would have wanted. By the time she died, Pete exceeded her track record as one of our most important donors.

Generally, if you wait until the children of your donors come into their family's money, it's too late – and far too transparent – to begin cultivating them for your cause. Even when their parents are alive and active, your approach must be creative.

One of my donors was interested in the arts. Judy's son, Henry, who was employed by a prominent financial institution, was not. Henry's philanthropic focus was education, especially the needs of at-risk kids. One day I had the opportunity to talk with him and our conversation turned to the challenge of helping poor children acquire the skills they need in the contemporary workforce.

"All this emphasis on memorization and testing is so often misguided," said Henry. "Much of what they're being taught will be irrelevant or simply wrong 10 years after they graduate. Then what? They need to be flexible and creative – they need to be able to problem-solve at a very high level. But that's not what they're learning."

I steered the conversation to various organizations that were helping schools deal with that deficiency by offering enrichment programs heavy on creativity. I mentioned how tests showed that these programs were successful in providing many of the workforce skills he identified.

Henry was fascinated and wanted to learn more. I sent him material and we talked about some opportunities that fit his guidelines for support. Judy and Henry ended up supporting many of the same organizations, albeit for very different reasons. Judy was thrilled – it gave her one more point of contact with her busy and successful son and enhanced her standing with the organizations she loved.

The opportunity of involving donors' children in actually developing philanthropic goals was something I came to believe was so important that I drilled the idea into my staff. I talked about it constantly and was always on the lookout for chances to put theory into practice. "Don't just ask the kids for money," I stressed. "Make them part of the fundraising team. If they give advice, chances are they'll give money."

Then one day, I was told about a new procedure our organization was implementing – direct withdrawal from donors' bank accounts. At the time, I wasn't familiar with the practice and was unsure whose idea it was to set it up. Our director of development explained: "Remember how you told us to seek advice from our donors' children? Well we did," she said impishly. "We approached your son. And you were right. Lex advised us to set up electronic funds transfer ... and gave us a nice gift too."

7

Can You Be Too Close to Ask?

Arthur and I were best friends in college. We took many of the same classes, had the same circle of friends, and spent hours obsessing about our love lives. Eventually we took an apartment together and grew even closer.

Within a year, we married women from our alma mater and the four of us continued to socialize. Eventually, when Arthur and his wife moved to another town, we bought their house.

A few years later, I was approached by a board member of an organization I was interested in helping. "Now's the time we need your assistance," he said to me. Arthur's name was mentioned. "You know him, right?"

"Of course I know him," I said.

"You know who he is, right?"

I knew vaguely that Arthur's mother had the same maiden name as a storied Fortune 500 corporation and that there was some connection. "Sort of," I said.

I was then regaled with a detailed history of his family and its wealth. "We want you to solicit Arthur for our capital campaign."

The thought completely threw me off stride. "I can't solicit him. He's my friend."

I quickly realized what I'd said and how silly it must have sounded. Of course he was my friend. That was the point. I had access. Any good fundraiser knows that tapping people with access is the name of the game. But I didn't want to use it. In the end, a close friendship trumped the opportunity for a large gift.

The story of Arthur points to a dilemma and an irony. Much of what an effective fundraiser does is leverage friendships. Organizations intentionally seek out solicitors with connections, the wider the better. But sometimes these relationships are so strong they actually get in the way of successful fundraising.

Consider my friend Martin. He was part of a notable family known for its generosity, the only member from my generation who appeared interested in the work of our organization.

I'd known him since childhood, though not

particularly well until my wife and I began to socialize with Martin and his wife. I told him one day that I'd love to talk about the work of our organization and he seemed willing. "Let's have a picnic at the house."

The day came and it was tremendous fun. Their house in the woods was on a meandering river far from any other houses. We swam in the afternoon. We talked about ourselves. The women joked about what it was like to marry into such large families with their range of "characters." We were having such a good time I found it hard to transition from what was a deepening friendship to an "ask."

And then Martin helped me out, giving me the cue I've used as a guidepost ever since. "Tom and I have a little business to conduct. We shouldn't be long. Don't eat all the deviled eggs before we get back."

With that simple remark, Martin showed me a way to separate friendship from the business of fundraising. And as I got to know him and his wife better, I realized they'd developed this strategy as a way of protecting their relationships. It was brilliant in its simplicity and it seemed to work for them.

Over the years, I've applied Martin's lesson. It involves two parts really: don't take friends by surprise, and do all you can to separate solicitation from friendship. Whether you secure the gift or not, you'll want to preserve your friendship. And almost always it is possible to do so.

Sometimes I've introduced the split ticket of friendship and soliciting with humor. "You're one of my prospects this year. Since I know you like to make me squirm, tell me when's the best time to chain me to the rack. Then we can go back to being normal."

Another approach I've used is the insider one. "Look, we have this new space that isn't going to be open to the public for awhile. I'm not supposed to encourage this kind of thing, but if you're willing to put on a hard hat, I can give you a private tour."

But what has become comfortable for me still unsettles many board members and volunteers. "I just can't do it," some say. "I'd rather solicit someone I don't know." It sounds reasonable, but of course it isn't. People give to people they know and assigning strangers to solicitors is a waste of talent. The alternative – asking board members and volunteers to open the door – is often recommended and is sound advice.

The problem of being too close to donors is something I used to think was unique to volunteers. I assumed that paid professionals wouldn't be afraid to cultivate donors and eventually solicit them. But I was wrong. Staff, too, can be so good at the friend-making process they become uncomfortable in their dual roles as friends and solicitors.

Some time ago I was consulting for a museum with a fine collection of drawings. The curatorial staff was encouraged to befriend important collectors and offer assistance. A collector, for instance, might be about to make an important purchase and want to know a curator's opinion of the work. "Offer to advise them," the museum director urged. "After all, any of these drawings may eventually end up in our collection."

Several curators enjoyed these outings. They became trusted confidents and friends of the collectors, often going to private homes to suggest how the drawings should be hung and sometimes going on exotic buying trips that extended into social occasions.

But when it came to discussing the eventual fate of the collectors' drawings, some of the curators balked. That wasn't part of the deal. One in particular felt uncomfortable. While he had perfect access to an important collector and was in a position to greatly assist in building the museum's collection, he felt it unseemly to do so. The two had become too close.

In the end, the problem was solved. This was a perfect opportunity for a pass-off. The director and another collector stepped in to do follow-up. They met with the donor, talked about how wonderful it had been for the curator to have the opportunity to be involved in such important purchases. "Well I should hope so," said the collector. "After all, your museum is going to get the pieces when I die. Better you should get stuff you really want."

As reported later, it was the easiest important ask the director had ever made, facilitated by someone else's friendship.

8

Why Isn't He Giving!?

Rob and his wife were among our organization's key donors. His wife's parents were in fact our very first contributors, providing a grant from their family foundation that proved helpful in securing other grants.

Through the years he was always a leadership donor, and though he declined to be interviewed for our campaign feasibility study, we weren't surprised. He shunned this sort of thing but we were confident.

We were so confident that we rated him as a top prospect with a gift of perhaps 10 percent to 15 percent of the total goal. Because of my long friendship with him, I was selected as his solicitor. Knowing he often preferred anonymity, I decided to do the "ask" by myself.

The visit started out as so many others with him had. We talked generally about economic trends, about his recent experiences chairing a capital campaign for the private school he attended as a boy, and what he saw as the motivations of different types of donors, especially those in the next generation.

We transitioned easily into my pitch. I knew what he'd be most interested in and focused his attention on it. I thought the presentation was worthy of a DVD I could use with my fundraising classes. Things were going as planned.

"I'm afraid the answer is no," Rob said, when I had finished.

Given my experience with this sort of meeting, I wasn't at all fazed. I prepared for what would be a negotiation. Clearly, the number I was suggesting was too high. I knew we could find the right level. Once again, I wished it were all being filmed. That was until Rob continued, "No, I won't be making a capital gift – not to you or anyone for awhile."

Rob told me of a confidential financial issue he was dealing with. Through no fault of his own, he was embroiled in a legal case that at worst could cost him a seven-figure sum and at best would probably involve him in considerable legal fees before it was resolved. "Of course, all this is confidential," he said, "but I really can't commit to anything now."

After overcoming my disappointment, I was faced

with two dilemmas: How do I proceed with Rob at this very moment and how do I prevent his refusal from undermining our morale, to say nothing of our campaign goal?

We may have taken on water, but I was determined we weren't going to sink. Rob still liked the organization, so I felt confident in exploring options. I reiterated the importance of the annual fund and asked that he consider making a larger gift in this area since it wasn't a multi-year commitment. I told him we would use it as a "challenge." Rob agreed and the first part of my task was accomplished.

"May I say that your position on the capital campaign is that now isn't a good time and that I can come back later when all this is resolved?" I asked. The answer again was "yes," and I felt that additional damage control had been accomplished. On the one hand, we retained Rob as a donor and on the other, his "no" to the campaign had significant wiggle room.

With Chuck, the outcome was the same – no gift from a key donor – but here I didn't have the opportunity to talk with him and explore options.

Chuck was among the wealthiest people in the community. He generally contributed to everything, including our organization, in a major way. But now he too refused to be interviewed for our feasibility study nor would he speak with any of us.

When he stopped giving completely, there was no explanation (though I learned later that someone in our organization made a remark he considered insulting). But all I and my trustees noticed was the prominent absence of Chuck's name on our donor list. And many other people noticed too. After all, he had historically been one of our major donors.

How does one handle such a situation, especially when so much of an organization's credibility rests upon those who support it, and when a major donor's refusal can have a domino effect on other would-be donors?

With Chuck, my first task was to reassure current donors. It wasn't unusual for big givers to take on many commitments and spread their money among different organizations, I told them. No one can support everything. I was confident they'd see Chuck's name once again among our donors.

That optimism and positive outlook, I felt, was itself part of a good fundraising strategy. All of us continued to be scrupulously polite to Chuck and his wife when we met them socially. And we decided a whole new approach was in order.

We turned to a young staffer who was working with our children's program and asked her to write to Chuck and his wife, describe the program, and appeal for their support. Knowing of Chuck's wife's interest in children, this approach seemed most sensible. And utilizing a young staff member who couldn't possibly be blamed for any previous misunderstanding was just the ticket. A contribution was forthcoming.

My third disappointment was Madelyn and her cautionary tale contains one of the great dangers for a fundraiser – feeling angry. Madelyn had recently divorced and remarried and her new husband was quite wealthy. With her first husband, she'd always made a contribution to our organization which, given their economic situation, I considered generous.

She came to many of our activities and professed great interest in our work. With the organization taking on a new project that I knew would interest her, and with Madelyn now having access to greater wealth, I went to see her and asked for $5,000. She said it sounded interesting and she'd discuss it with her husband.

A week later I received a letter explaining that with two children in college, things were a bit tight and they wouldn't be making the gift. I was surprised and a little disappointed, but let it go. After all, it is a mantra of fundraising that we should never count the money in other people's pockets. Perhaps there was less there than I thought.

But when I took my car in for service the next week, that changed. I asked the dealer, an old friend, how things were going. He happened to mention Madelyn and her new husband and how in the last year they'd bought two new cars – in cash – one of them a luxury sedan.

I was livid. Here was one of my long-time donors, now affluent, and crying poor. Of course, I was making all sorts of assumptions. Even though wealthy, perhaps Madelyn and her new husband *were* overextended, what with the purchase of two new cars and impending tuitions. Or perhaps her husband didn't care for our organization and had persuaded Madelyn that another was more deserving in his mind.

But I was in no mood for rationalizations. I went to the development committee and spewed forth various invectives. Their reaction surprised me. "Tom, you're no longer rational about this," they said. "You're too upset. We'll take them off your list and give them to someone else."

It was good advice. In real life, when our friends disappoint and anger us, we can move on. But in the world of fundraising, we cannot afford to. We need to figure out a way to continue the relationships or our organizations will be seriously impoverished.

To this day, I'm resentful about Madelyn. But another solicitor, absent the long history with Madelyn, is securing gifts each year from her. I suspect they'll never be as large as I think they should, but what I think no longer matters.

In the end, wealthy and important donors will say "no" to us for any number of reasons just as any friend may turn us down when we ask a favor. How we handle those refusals will help determine whether they're serious breaches in important relationships or, preferably, simply temporary setbacks.

9

When Donors Disappoint

Kay was probably the most colorful person I'd ever met. She began her professional life as a model and was featured on the covers of *Life Magazine*, *Ladies Home Journal*, and other magazines.

Later, she went into films playing, as her biography in Wikipedia puts it, "feisty and frequently-imperiled heroines." Though she retired from pictures the year I was born, there was no question about her stardom and celebrity when I knew her years later – at least not in our town where she lived with her second husband, a wealthy artist.

Kay lived well. She was often seen around town in her Rolls Royce and entertained at her mansion overlooking the sea. She was a special draw at local fundraising events and occasionally served as celebrity auctioneer.

When I began my fundraising career, Kay was high on my prospect list and I had the perfect way to involve her or so I thought. At the time, the music organization I worked for held receptions following every performance.

Each event had a community hostess who was responsible for providing refreshments and greeting those who attended. The venue was the small parish house at a local church that conveniently provided kitchen facilities and the necessary dishes, table clothes, and silverware. The hostesses either prepared the refreshments themselves or arranged for catering. The expectation was that each hostess would sign up to become one of the organization's patrons at the same time, thereby attracting others to do so.

I made an appointment to see Kay and was thrilled to be invited to her house for an 11 a.m. meeting. When I arrived she wasn't at home and I was told to wait. For an hour and a half, I sat out on the porch with a magazine until Kay breezed in. I had the distinct impression she'd forgotten our appointment, had no idea why I was there, and maybe, just maybe, didn't even know who I was. Nevertheless, none of that mattered. Kay talked and talked. The star quality was still there and I was agog.

I finally blurted out why I'd come and she readily agreed to everything I requested with an offhand "of course, of course." It seemed beneath her to discuss small details so I was brief. And she clearly had other things on her mind. She spoke at length about her teenage daughter who had just arrived from somewhere in the south. "She doesn't know a soul here and I'm sure she'd love to have dinner with you – are you free tonight?" Caught off guard, I said yes and Kay proceeded to stuff several large bills in my pocket and said she'd make a reservation at a local eatery.

The dinner was enjoyable but over the next few days I had the unsettling feeling that Kay hadn't really taken in the purpose of my visit. Just to be sure, I followed up with a detailed letter. "If there is any problem or you have any questions," I wrote, "please let me know." Hearing nothing, I arranged for a corsage to be sent to Kay the night of the event with a reminder of when we looked forward to seeing her.

The night of the event I was encouraged. Kay arrived on time and looked dazzling. She greeted many of our star-struck guests and everything was going well. I did notice the kitchen was empty and marveled at the caterer she must have hired who could pull things together so quickly. By intermission, however, I knew there was a problem. Still no kitchen activity. And when I asked Kay about it she seemed confused. "I'm not sure what you mean," she said. Clearly, if there was to be any food or drink that evening, we needed a miracle.

And she arrived in the form of my older sister. It turned

out Sani was hosting a party the next day and had already purchased the refreshments. She rushed home, while others heated the water for coffee and tea, and still others set the tables. As the final strains of music were fading away, the room was magically transformed. Kay presided like a queen, accepting everyone's thanks for a lovely evening. And as I thanked her as well, I realized the promised patron check would never come.

Some would say I should have been grateful – after all we did get from Kay what she uniquely could give – her star quality and gracious manner. And I suppose it did help. People signed up to support us in the end and for years afterwards people remembered Kay's evening. But I felt as if I'd failed. Kay had neither done the hostessing nor given the gift I'd hoped for.

With Mike I wasn't as "fortunate."

Mike had built a successful insurance business and bragged a lot about his philanthropy. I decided to call his bluff and approached him for an endowment gift that would honor his best friend, who had been the board president of the organization I worked for at the time.

Mike was enthusiastic. He promised me $50,000 but was a little vague about the payment schedule. Always one to put things in writing, I sent him a letter confirming our conversation and suggesting a payment schedule and a date for the announcement of the gift. When I didn't hear back, I assumed we had a deal and announced the new fund. Big mistake!

I'd never gotten Mike's signature on any document. He had sounded so certain in our conversation that I'd decided not to push it. Three months later when the first pledge payment didn't arrive, Mike turned scarce. He didn't return phone calls, didn't answer letters. It was like our conversation never happened, and I never saw a dime of the committed money.

So the question is, what do you do when all the good work and time invested in fundraising and friend-raising fails? What do you do about the Kays and the Mikes of the world? As with any frustrating effort, your instinct is to get mad and tell them what you think of their behavior. Satisfying it may be, but prudent it isn't.

My friend, Gigi Antoni, the CEO of Big Thought (a creative learning organization in Dallas) has another way. She calls it "bless and release," which I've always found a wonderful mantra. When it's clear a person isn't going to support you – either with money or anything else – thank them and graciously let go. "You never know," says Gigi. "They might – just might – become your biggest supporters at some point!"

I certainly learned that lesson with Lillian, the final character in this chapter of frustrations. Lillian was another colorful character. She was never in films like Kay, but she was clever, talented, and funny. After restoring an 18th century farmhouse with her husband, Lillian looked around for something else to do. Her new occupation, she decided, would be a bookshop owner specializing in rare books.

Lillian had an efficient system for valuing books. She waited until a seemingly knowledgeable customer brought in a pile of books for purchase. Pleading that she'd left her price list at home, she'd ask the customer to call the next day. When he left Lillian would immediately begin researching which books had value and which didn't. The next day she was prepared with an aggressive pricing schedule from which to haggle. I knew the system. I was one of her victims.

Just as Lillian was difficult to predict and tie down when it came to pricing books, getting a fundraising commitment from her was equally challenging. She did give an annual gift, but when it came to anything more – most especially a large capital gift – she was cagey. I spent many hours working hard for such a gift and during her lifetime was never able to secure one. I was frustrated but continued to be pleasant and moved on.

Lillian died a few years after I'd stopped asking her for money. I didn't know whether she had any heirs nor did I know what she'd done with her money. I had pretty much lost interest. Imagine my surprise when a letter arrived from a law firm informing us that our organization was to receive a significant slice of her estate.

In my mind, I thanked Lillian and told her she'd gotten the last laugh and won the final round. And I reminded myself: "Always be polite. You simply never know!"

10

Recovering from a Fumble

I'd always liked Bart. We'd been friends in college. He led a Bohemian life style I envied. Visiting his off-campus apartment – filled with people day and night – always meant a good time.

Bart's attitude toward life was "devil-may-care" and that included his finances. Chronically short of cash and filled with big ideas, he constantly hit on us. But that was okay. Bart maintained our "clubhouse" and it was our membership fee.

However, 20 years later Bart's unremitting need for funds and his inability to follow through on any of his money-making projects had lost their charm. I stayed in touch as he went through several marriages, had children, moved constantly, and never seemed able to hold a job. As Bart's requests for money continued and the sums grew larger, I lost interest and the friendship petered out.

I was thinking of Bart the afternoon I approached an important prospect, Bill, for a six-figure gift to our endowment. Bill was evasive at first, detailing his frustration with another organization on whose board he sat. To him, their requests for money seemed as frequent as Bart's and their ability to use it wisely about as rare.

"Last year, I gave them the exact amount you're asking for," he told me. "I wanted to give it to their endowment but they were in trouble so I said they could use it for operations IF they'd get their house in order. They promised to do so.

"There was euphoria that the year would end in the black. But guess what? The bookkeeper recorded the gift twice. And no one caught the error. Imagine everyone's embarrassment, especially mine, when we discovered we were in the red – a whopping $150,000. To make things worse, I'm on the Finance Committee!"

I hate to say it, but that organization's poor stewardship lost them a donor and gained me a friend – a friend who over time became one of our largest donors. Stewardship, in the end, counted a lot for Bill. I continued to show him how we used his gifts. I made reports available. I introduced Bill to people who benefited directly from his generosity. And he continued to be a donor well into his nineties.

Alas, in a strangely similar situation, I dropped the ball with another donor some years later. I've always prided myself as being someone whom my donor friends can rely on for impeccable stewardship. So it was with a sense of dread that I landed in the hot seat.

I made an appointment to speak with my friend and board member, Pete, whom I mentioned earlier, about a shortfall in our own finances. It was particularly embarrassing. Pete had made a $50,000 unrestricted gift to our endowment just two months before. That was close to the amount we were going to be short in the operating budget.

While technically, we weren't going to touch his money and it would remain in the endowment, we'd still take an equal amount from our reserves to cover the shortfall. This was a bit like literally robbing Pete to pay Paul. The net result of his gift to the organization's net worth was exactly zero. He was effectively paying for our poor stewardship.

As I drove to his house, I planned carefully what I'd say. Since Pete was a friend as well as a donor, I thought about the best way to approach a friend whom you've let down. Talk to him directly, look him in the eye, admit your mistake, explain exactly what happened, and tell him how you'll make sure it doesn't happen again.

"Look, Pete," I said once we were seated face-to-face. "We've not done as well as we'd hoped this year financially. I can explain where we fell short and why we did, but that's not the point. You trusted me and I didn't deliver. I came here to talk about it."

Pete, always interested in the numbers, wanted to see them and understand what had happened. We talked for over an hour. Each time we reviewed where the numbers had gone awry, I had an explanation. It didn't make the results any easier to swallow but at least I had the facts and figures at my fingertips.

"I'm disappointed," said Pete. "No question about that. But it isn't so much about the shortfall – that happens to organizations. What disappoints me is that we didn't see this coming. Why not? Weren't there any signs?"

Pete was right, of course. It was my fault, even if he was reluctant to finger me. I had seen the possibility of problems as early as six months before. But I stayed quiet, hoping things would improve.

Having learned my lesson, I watch our financial results like a hawk today. When I see numbers materializing in a way I didn't anticipate, I let people know – the Treasurer, Finance Committee, and key donors whose gifts might be affected. I warn of possible outcomes that may require an adjustment in our planning.

Usually things pan out better than my warnings suggest. But I find that several of my donor friends, many of whom are financially savvy people, welcome the honesty. Often they tell me not to worry. Occasionally they suggest adjustments in our spending. Their requirement is not that we be perfect, but that we're responsible, forthright, and open.

And when you think about it, aren't those the same obligations of a lasting friendship?

11

But I Can't Stand the Fellow!

There was no question Stephen had money – lots of money. The way he threw it around when he came to town, there was no mistaking the fact that he intended to use his largesse to establish his clout. I had little to do with him until one day he phoned. He'd heard about the work of our organization and had an idea. He thought it would be very worth my while to meet with him.

Since Stephen was the talk of our small town, I mentioned to a few people that I was going to see him and the response was always the same: "Be careful." But I wasn't especially worried. Being relatively young in my fundraising career, I had the overconfidence that comes with lack of experience. I was simply going to meet Stephen, have a tour of his renovated house, and hear him out. That was all. I knew how to deal with people like him and I knew how to say "no."

I visited Stephen and was impressed with his house, one of the most historic in town. But once he started talking about himself, discomfort set in. He spent a lot of time telling me about his seven homes, his private plane, his two sailboats each with its own crew. He told me the prices he paid for each work of art on the wall and about how many so-called art connoisseurs were "idiots." He was the kind of fellow to whom I take an instant dislike ... but he had money, and he was making it clear that if I played my cards right I could have some.

In retrospect, I cringe at my behavior. I was friendly, feigned interest, and expressed admiration where the cues were obvious. Later I professed friendship and went to his house when summoned. In the end, my organization received his money, one of our largest gifts ever. I was cautiously pleased and so were my trustees.

But no sooner did we receive his gift than I got a lot else besides. Phone calls came at unexpected hours filled with advice, much of it impractical or downright loony. Conversations were often spiced with derogatory comments about friends and associates I respected. I wanted to rebut Stephen but felt awkward, and then felt even worse about my cowardice for not doing so. At the end of the year, he offered even more money, and I had to make a decision. Was it really worth it? I went to some valued trustees to seek their advice.

Interestingly, the board was split. One of my trustees, old and wise, said we should take the money and not worry about it. "So you have to put up with some bizarre behavior. It's part of your job." He recalled a similar situation on another board where the headmaster came to him complaining about a donor whose money was gained in a shady manner. "It's tainted money," said the headmaster, "and it doesn't feel right." My board member shot back: "The only tainted money is the money we taint got."

But the majority of my trustees felt differently. They saw how uncomfortable I was. More importantly, there was growing talk in the community and among other donors that this wasn't a good situation for us. Stephen had a checkered reputation. They urged me to walk away and in the end I did so, leaving a large sum on the table.

My experience with Stephen points to a dilemma about our relationships with some of our donors. Good fundraisers have to be willing to be friends with their donors and to build strong relationships. But should we play nice with people we really can't stand? How authentic are we if our "friends" include people like Stephen? Or should we simply admit that these efforts are manipulative ploys to secure money and not worry about it? What is our responsibility to our organizations, to the donors, and most importantly to ourselves?

Most wealthy people have learned to be cautious toward those of us who profess to be their friends. When we behave inexplicably, as I did with Stephen, they can only suspect one thing – it IS all about the money.

As one donor whom I asked to join my table at a fundraiser said out of the blue, "My husband told me tonight, 'Watch out, they're just after your money. They'll pretend to be your friend but just know what they are after.' He says that to me all the time and I wish he wasn't right about it so often."

Sitting next to her I felt odd. Sure we wanted a gift from her. But I thought the evening was fun for both of us and we were having a good time. Should I have felt guilty?

Everyone is suspicious of the sycophant who lavishes praise in advance of asking for money. But what of the fundraiser who goes about the process with subtlety and skill? Should we be even more on our guard? Is there any way to tell when people are being authentic?

This, perhaps, is the crux of the issue. When we're inauthentic, donors can tell. But the opposite is true as well. When we act with integrity, it comes across, especially as donors come to know us.

My friend, Andrea Kihlstedt, an exceptional fundraiser in her own right, makes an interesting and important distinction. "We can be kind and gracious in the face of challenging behavior. That's okay. But we shouldn't try to become everyone's friend or pretend we enjoy working with donors who are troublesome. In the end, maintaining our integrity may be the most important thing that keeps us from growing cynical."

I agree wholeheartedly.

12

Whose Friend Are You Anyway?

When I hired Charles, I was concerned he might be too young and, not from the community, have difficulty getting to know people. Would he fit into an organization where the demographic of the donors was older and many had known each other for years?

I needn't have worried – at least about that. Charles took to some of our key donors right away and they were drawn to him. He established a small committee to assist him and they seemed enthusiastic about him and his work ethic.

Charles had a girlfriend, Evelyn, with a fundraising background. When Charles came to town, she moved with him, though she didn't have a job. It wasn't long before she landed a development post. I was happy. It meant Charles would be more committed to staying in town.

But then I began to notice something troubling. The ranks of new donors in Evelyn's organization were filling up with some familiar names – names of our donors! I chalked it up to living in a small town. Of course there'd be overlap – that happens even in large cities. I surmised that Evelyn was simply doing remedial work for an organization whose development operation was being upgraded.

But then I was given greater pause. At the end of the year, Charles and I and some other staff were reviewing a list of lapsed donors and we came to the name of a long-time $1,000 per year donor. "Oh, John isn't going to give to us this year," said Charles. "He's giving his $1,000 to Evelyn's group."

"How do you know?" I asked.

"Well, we took him out for a drink the other night and he told us."

Suddenly, danger lights flashed. What's going on here? Charles was my employee. His loyalty was supposed to be to our organization. Sure, I encouraged him to be friendly with our donors. Going out for a drink was okay – even good, if it helped us. But if this was merely an opportunity to help Evelyn gain a donor, it wasn't okay – especially if it happened at our expense.

I asked to see Charles later in the day and confronted him. He seemed unfazed and a little surprised. "You encouraged me to make friends with donors. I have. Sometimes that means going out for a drink. And often Evelyn will be with me. John asked about her new job and she told him. He was intrigued and decided to give his $1,000 to her. I can't control his behavior."

Over time, I've learned that encouraging staff and trustees to make friends with donors is often double-edged. It can pay dividends if trustees and staff are loyal. But it can also work against you if they're not – or if they have other personal or professional interests complicating the relationship.

While we can hold a staff member accountable if he or she gives a mailing list away or provides other proprietary information, the kinds of things that may pass between friends constitute a grey area that, as Charles pointed out, give little room for calling someone on the carpet.

Consider the case of Katherine – another of my staff who spent a good deal of time running our development operation. When she left, it was for a good reason. She was courted and eventually hired by a competitor that offered her the top job. Having given her a lavish recommendation, I celebrated her success.

But Katherine carried with her not only the

knowledge she had acquired about our donors, but also several relationships that she had nurtured at my insistence. Four months after she was hired, one of my long-time donors mentioned he was reducing his gift to us. When I asked why, he said Katherine's organization needed the money more.

The situation is even more problematic when a staff member leaves the organization under less than happy circumstances. Katherine continued to be a good colleague and was as sensitive to the situation as I was, much to her credit. She wanted to stay in my good graces and I in hers. But if the leave-taking is acrimonious, there's often no such restraint.

Is there any foolproof method for avoiding these situations? Can an organization prevent these kinds of practices? After decades of doing this work, my simple answer is "no." If people want to abuse their loyalty by taking advantage of friendships developed as a result of their association with your organization, they'll find a way to do so.

On the other hand, I've found two things that help – both simple. One is to be clear in writing about the organization's ethics, standards, and expectations when people join – whether board or staff. The second is to develop and celebrate a standard of behavior that discourages people from deviating from it. Pride in being part of an organization known for its integrity is often a powerful incentive itself.

13

We Honor His Memory

My brother Andy was a concert pianist. At the age of 40, he was enjoying a distinguished career, at times playing Carnegie Hall. His specialty was chamber music and performing as a collaborating pianist with classical music stars.

Then illness struck in the form of a brain tumor. As Andy's end drew near, numerous people said to me and to other family members that something should be done to honor his memory. At the time, our focus was clearly elsewhere and we put off making any decisions.

But then Albert stepped forward and asked to see us a few months *before* Andy's death. Albert was an elderly music lover, philanthropist, and a board member of the concert series Andy had founded. He loved Andy as a son (he'd lost his own son some years earlier) and asked whether our family might approve of a musical prize being set up in Andy's memory.

Albert's sensitivity was remarkable. He would only proceed with the family's blessing and he was prepared to make the first gift – a large one. He wondered whether others – including some from the family and from the music school Andy ran in Boston – would join him. He asked us to think about it and to let him know our ideas and our decision.

The story of how the Andrew Wolf Chamber Music Award was created and endowed is an inspiring one. The award was made possible by a committed and sensitive donor, good planning, a willing fundraising team, and a project that was commensurate with the amount that could be raised. It also depended on an organization ready and willing to do advance planning on short notice.

It might seem strange to talk about advance planning when the subject is a memorial gift. But think about it. The majority of deaths aren't unexpected even in the case of a relatively young person. In some instances, the individual to be memorialized may even have his or her own ideas about how a fund could be established and for what purpose. Why then, are so many organizations so unprepared to help families and other donors who may be thinking of a memorial?

Some of it owes to our discomfort with mortality, most especially our own but others' as well. Then too, many organizations lack sensitive staff and volunteers who can sit and talk comfortably with those experiencing the loss. Albert, as a member of the board of the concert organization, was just the right person. Because of the death of his own son, he knew what the family was going through.

But being prepared involves more than interpersonal skills. An organization needs clear guidelines, as these can help align expectations with reality. Many people connected with a dying or deceased individual can be unrealistic about how much can be raised in a memorial situation and how much an organization should be willing to do for that amount. Our family certainly didn't know.

An organization is far better prepared when it determines rationally and in advance a sensible giving hierarchy for memorial gifts. As an example, an organization might say that gifts totaling less than $5,000 will go automatically into its annual fund with no strings attached. A total gift pool of between $5,000 and $25,000 can be restricted (commensurate with the organization's regular activities) but will also be spent within the current fiscal year or the next. Only with total gifts of $25,000-

plus to this hypothetical organization could the family ask that the dollars go into the endowment for a restricted purpose – and a list of possible categories of endowment gifts would be ready to show families. Armed with this kind of information, a conversation with an individual or a family (or a well-meaning donor) can be based on facts and figures.

While gifts of this kind will be infrequent in most organizations, from my own experience when they're handled well similar gifts may follow. People who are pleased will talk to their friends – often other donors – and this will plant a seed.

As you would expect, not every memorial situation is smooth. A friend of mine told me that his family was approached when his brother died. A faculty member of the deceased's high school asked whether the family would be willing to have a building named after him. Nothing was said about money and the family was perhaps too naive (or not lucid enough in a moment of grief) to realize they were being asked for more than their agreement.

A month after consenting, a member of the development staff called to follow up about the family's "commitment." The misunderstanding caused heartache on both sides and as of this writing the building remains unnamed.

There is one last situation connected with memorials that's fraught with danger. It's when a grieving family approaches an organization and asks that a named memorial be established.

A colleague of mine described a situation where a donor wanted to memorialize his daughter. "The concept wasn't consistent with our mission, the family was only going to give a small amount of the money, and we were to do all the work. To make it worse, the rest of their family was off-limits as prospects. I wish I could say we bowed out gracefully and kept our donor. Unfortunately, we handled it poorly and the family was offended in the process."

Had the institution developed a set of guidelines in advance, indicating how much money would be required to establish different types of memorials, it would have been on much more solid ground. It would have helped the grieving family understand that there are existing systems in place for these situations, even when the individual is beloved by all.

14

Grantmakers Need Attention Too

My friend, Carole Brand, leads a charmed life ... or so I decided recently when she told me of her grantseeking experience. Retired after a successful career in the business world, she's smart, effective, and generous. Everyone likes this special woman.

At the time, Carole was board chair of a small nonprofit – a rural chapter of Literacy Volunteers of America. Though experienced in nonprofit governance, this was the first time she'd been affiliated with an organization without fundraising staff.

Along with another board member who agreed to research foundations, Carole rolled up her sleeves and decided to write a proposal. The two of them identified a funder that appeared to have criteria matching those

99

of Literacy Volunteers. After reviewing the guidelines, Carole submitted a proposal asking for roughly 60 percent of the organization's annual budget.

A few months later, a letter arrived from the foundation. Carole hoped it contained some good news, but even she wasn't holding out for 60 percent of the budget. Instead, what the letter said was almost too good to believe. Literacy Volunteers was doing such important work the foundation would give them everything they'd asked for. Mirabile dictu – a grantmaker showering Carole with more money than she could have ever expected.

The only person I know who can outdo this experience is another friend I mentioned earlier, Barbara Bentley, head of the board of The Friends of Baxter State Park. A foundation had fully funded the first year of a three-year project. When the Friends reapplied in year two, the response was extraordinary. They not only received full funding but an extra 50 percent was tacked onto the check.

What's going on here? What is Carole's and Barbara's special secret? Actually it's very simple. Natural intuition told these two women there were real live people behind these grants – people with opinions and feelings. What they wrote was compelling and spoke to the human aspects of their projects. In each case someone paid particular attention.

Of course, they were lucky too. Countless grantwriters craft heartfelt prose and don't get funded. But as someone who has worked in a foundation for years, I know that certain proposals stand out and they're not the ones cut and pasted or assembled by formula.

I related these stories to a grantmaker friend and asked for her reaction. "Let's start with the basics," she said. "A grant-giving entity, whether it's a government agency, a corporation, or a foundation, is an organization made up of people – sometimes one person, sometimes hundreds.

"From the moment someone decides to seek funding, the focus has to be on the people who'll make the decision. Who are they? What can you learn about them? What excites them? What kinds of organizations are they funding and for what? Is there a pattern? Is there some way you (or a member of your board or a volunteer) can get access to them? Is there a strategy to build a relationship?

"When I was on the other side, I had a general rule. I tried not to submit a proposal until I'd talked with someone at the foundation or company I was applying to. And if there was any chance of meeting an individual face-to-face, I'd put off submitting a proposal, often for months, until I had that meeting."

Most funding officers, whether they work at foundations, corporations, or in government, have limited time, if any, to meet with applicants. They grow impatient and grumpy when you haven't done your homework. I myself spent seven years as a foundation executive and nothing bothered me so much as people who'd call for an appointment, but hadn't read a description of what we funded or reviewed our guidelines. "Never ask a question that can be answered by our existing literature," I'd counsel them.

I was much more receptive when someone said, "We're excited after reading about your foundation. We've reviewed your guidelines and looked at the projects you've funded recently. But we're still not sure which of the ideas we're considering might have the best chance of success."

This kind of an approach would immediately pique my curiosity and put me in the frame of mind I liked best – I could steer them toward a project I felt was most worthy, suggest something else as I learned about the organization, or counsel them not to apply if it all seemed too far-fetched.

There's another important rationale for gaining access to the people behind the scenes. In times past, foundations simply waited to see what applications came in and then made decisions accordingly. This so-called "responsive" philanthropy was the dominant method of grantmaking. Many still do this of course. But a different approach – "initiative" grantmaking – is becoming the norm today.

Here the method is different. Grantmakers identify an area they want to fund – say community-based wellness programs – and locate nonprofit partners they think will do the best job in addressing this priority. There's no application process for this first round. Instead, proposals are invited from a pre-selected group. If the grantmaker has never heard of you, you're out of luck. But if you've made yourself known, if you've somehow penetrated the veil of the foundation, obviously your chances are much enhanced.

And now we come to one of the trickiest parts of the process – determining who really calls the shots and to whom you should be addressing your appeals, your questions, and your friend-making efforts. In a small foundation, it's generally easy. There are thousands of these entities. They're often extensions of family fortunes and it's pretty clear who is deciding. But as the grantmaking institutions grow in size, it's easy to make a mistake – and a mistake can prove fatal.

Some time ago a colleague and I were working on a major proposal to a national foundation. Our contact was a program officer named Merrill who seemed to be speaking for the decision-makers. He gave detailed information – even confiding to us some of the internal deliberations of the trustees.

Merrill liked us, we liked him, and we followed his instructions to the letter. A few weeks before we were to submit our proposal, the foundation overhauled its guidelines, and I panicked. We were caught unprepared so I called Merrill. "This is very different than what we anticipated," I said. "Should we adjust our proposal?"

"No, don't worry," he assured us. "You're fine. We've specifically set aside money for proposals like yours."

We submitted the proposal and were turned down. The next day we called Merrill.

"You know, you really should have followed the new guidelines," he said. "The trustees were hardly going to spend all this effort revamping the guidelines only to have people like you not follow them."

We were astonished. Dr. Jekyll had become Mr. Hyde.

A week later I spoke to a friend about this. "Oh that's typical," he said. "The board jealously guards its power and program directors scurry around trying to interpret what they're supposed to say and do. When they make a mistake, as Merrill apparently did, they rarely admit it. It makes them look bad ... and weak. It would have been better if you tried to establish a board contact."

In this case, I did know a board member and could have called him. But I decided against it. When you go over the head of staff, you can easily make a long-term enemy. As important, you really have no idea of the organizational politics involved and run the real risk of forming an alliance with the wrong person or faction. Lastly, it's not uncommon for board members themselves to be unclear about the foundation's priorities, and thus offer you misguided advice. Still, I knew this particular board member well and in retrospect feel the risks would have been worth it.

Another concern in reading the politics of a foundation is to ignore someone at the bottom of the organizational chart. Once I was consulting for a grantmaker and asked if I could sit in on a grants session with the staff.

Six people assembled and I was surprised to see the receptionist at the table. I assumed she'd be taking minutes but in fact she participated in the meeting, often expressing her opinions forthrightly. At one point, a proposal was under discussion about an outreach project from a local organization. "You wouldn't believe how rude these people were every time they called or came in," she said.

"Well that's not good," said the foundation's director. "If they're only interested in kowtowing to people they think have power, how are they going to be effective at outreach?"

The proposal wasn't funded and I learned an important lesson. Everyone deserves courtesy and special attention.

AFTERWORD

In this book I've given you suggestions for connecting with donors. If you follow the advice, I believe you'll draw many of your donors and potential donors closer to you.

But as we all know, we're drawn to various people for complicated reasons, many of which we can't and don't even try to identify. Will you find a best friend among your donors? Probably not. Besides, getting *too* close to donors can actually thwart your money-raising efforts as we've seen.

But can you cultivate a number of dear acquaintances with whom you'll socialize? Absolutely.

In these pages I've written about my friend Pete, a long-time donor, and it's with him I'll close this book. Had it not been for his mother, I doubt I would have spent much time with Pete. But as Elsie aged, he took over her finances and we grew close. When she died, Pete took her place among our most important donors. He also became a mentor, a champion, and, when appropriate, a critic.

At first I didn't like that last part. Pete fancied himself a curmudgeon and was quite comfortable voicing his disapproval when he felt we were veering off track. Sometimes I agreed. Sometimes I disagreed. And there were times when he drove me crazy.

Then Pete contracted a virus. Doctors couldn't diagnose the problem – apparently he picked up a bug in his travels. Pete couldn't eat, he lost weight, and grew very weak. Suddenly I realized, "I love this guy."

I went into high gear cooking up exotic fare, hoping something would appeal to his appetite. His illness went on for weeks. But fortunately Pete came through and credited my cuisine in part for his recovery.

It was philanthropy that threw Pete and me together. He's someone I never would have met but for his mother. But as you've learned by now, I make it my business to involve a donor's family in important decisions. So here's a clear case where fundraising "technique," the kind I espouse in this book, led directly to friendship.

Some people when they confront death are changed forever. Those escaping a near-fatal car crash often tell you that their priorities have changed forever. Well, Pete wasn't that close to the grim reaper and as his strength returned he was only too happy to continue his curmudgeonly ways. He hadn't changed a bit.

One day as we were reviewing the budget, he said, "Tell the folks who come up with these foolish ideas we have to pay for them. Or should I personally go show 'em what a dollar bill looks like?"

Ah, Pete is Pete, I thought. He continued to be one of our key donors ... and amiable critics. "Oh well," I mused, "That's friendship, isn't it."

It certainly is. And I'll take it – all of it – quite happily.

ABOUT THE AUTHOR

Dr. Thomas Wolf's career encompasses the fields of philanthropy, nonprofit management, education, and the arts.

After serving as the founding Director of the New England Foundation for the Arts for seven years, he established a consulting firm in 1983 (now called WolfBrown) to assist nonprofit organizations and the philanthropic sector.

Helping his clients increase fundraising results and improve management practices, he also assisted 10 of the 50 largest U.S. foundations and various government agencies with their grants programs.

At the same time, his workshops and convocations for trustees, administrators, and volunteers have earned him national recognition.

Wolf holds a doctorate in education from Harvard, and has taught at Harvard and Boston Universities. He is the author of the definitive textbook on nonprofit management that has been in print for over a quarter century (now titled *Managing a Nonprofit Organization in the 21st Century*) and he has written numerous other books and articles.

A professional flutist whose career included touring with the Goldovsky Opera Theatre and founding Bay Chamber Concerts in Maine, he is currently listed in the International Who's Who of Music.

Copies of this and other books from the
publisher are available at discount when
purchased in quantity for boards of directors
or staff. Call 508-359-0019 or visit
www.emersonandchurch.com